ROLLER SKATING

ROLLER SKATING

BY D. J. HERDA

FRANKLIN WATTS
NEW YORK | LONDON | 1979
A FIRST BOOK

Cover and frontis photograph courtesy of
the Roller Skating Rink Operators Association

Other photographs by the author

Drawings by Vantage Art, Inc.

Library of Congress Cataloging in Publication Data

Herda, D   J   1948–
Roller skating.

(A First book)
Includes index.
SUMMARY: A history of roller skating with in-
structions for the beginning skater, directions for
group games on skates, and information on competitive skating.
1. Roller skating—Juvenile literature.   2. Roller
skating—History—Juvenile literature.   [1. Roller
skating] I. Title.
GV859.H47   796.2′1   78–11043
ISBN 0–531–02262–5

CONTENTS

Special thanks for their help in preparing this book go to Suzi Theis of the Roller Skating Rink Operators Association and to the owners, operators, and employees of the Rollerdrome and The Wheel Thing roller rinks in Madison, Wisconsin. And very special thanks go to Malisa Price, one of the finest young skaters I know.

ROLLER SKATING

DISCO DAYS

A rare old photograph in the collection of the Sioux City, Iowa, Public Museum depicts the early days of roller skating. The photo, taken in the 1880s, shows women in ankle-length skirts and men dressed in suits, stiff white shirts, and ties. Thirty or forty people are standing in a huge hall with exposed rafters and decorated with American flags. They are enjoying a day of skating at the Goldie Roller Skating Rink in Sioux City.

Times have changed since then. Walk into today's roller skating rink and you're likely to see people in jeans and T-shirts. Those with skates on are doing jazzy steps out on the floor. And those with skates off are doing just as jazzy routines around a jukebox in the back.

Many of today's most successful rinks have thrown off their conservative look and dressed up in a rainbow of hues and textures. Carpeting lines the floor around the rink, often climbing up the walls to the ceiling. The harsh glare of a white spotlight trained on the middle of the room has been replaced by a whirl of soft-glow psychedelic lighting, spiraling out in all directions.

Gone from the modern roller skating rink are the exposed rafters, the open, boxlike feel of the room, often even the traditional wooden floor. The rink of the 1970s—such as Skate World in Tulsa, Oklahoma—offers a gleaming plastic floor that is less costly to install and easier to care for than wood.

There is even a new sound to roller skating, a new beat that has captured the imagination of roller skaters everywhere. It's called roller disco, and it's the latest craze to sweep America.

Roller disco is more than just a fad. It's disco music set to wheels, the start of a whole new era. The thirties had jazz. The fifties saw the rise of rock and roll, and the sixties popularized folk music. But the seventies have witnessed the explosion of the music industry with a sound that goes beyond the ears and enters the very heart of the listener—the disco sound.

Not surprisingly, disco music has invaded skating rinks across the country. Today, roller skaters gather regularly—especially in larger cities—to perform their own dances. But, unlike the waltz, fox-trot, and tango performed on skates in years past, today's roller skate dances are modern, upbeat flings that leave wheels spinning.

One of the newer attractions of today's roller skating rink is a live disc jockey providing the disco sound to skaters.

Such disco groups as Earth, Wind & Fire, K C & the Sunshine Band, and the Ohio Players lead the field in roller disco. Many roller rink operators have taken advantage of disco-dancing crowds by not only playing the music, but also creating a disco atmosphere. Bright lights and sleek fixtures line ceilings and walls. More effective sound systems throw off pulsing, exciting dance beats.

Tulsa's Skate World offers a good example of the changes that have taken place in roller skating over the last ten years. It offers 24,000 square feet (2,230 sq m) of pleasure, featuring a mod atmosphere of stereophonic disco music, flashing lights, and supergraphics. In addition to the fun of skating, visitors there may enjoy freshly baked pizza or hot chocolate at the snack bar, or even spend time playing electronic football or hockey at the brand-new $50,000 game complex in a corner nearby.

But the changes in the world of roller skating consist of more than these innovations in lighting, music, and decorations. There has been a complete change in the way people think of roller skating. Let's see why.

Another popular feature of the modern roller skating rink is a game area for between skating periods.

1

THE BIRTH OF A SPORT

No one knows for sure who invented roller skating. Legend has it that it was probably a man, that the man lived in Holland in the eighteenth century, that he was an ice skater, and that he loved the sport.

No one knows for sure exactly how it happened either. Perhaps one day, after walking down to the canal where he ice-skated most often, the inventor of roller skating noticed something unusual. There were no skaters on the ice. Upon drawing nearer, the reason became apparent. The canal—which only the day before had been frozen solid—was beginning to melt. The ice was soft and no longer strong enough to support any weight.

So the man turned sadly away and began the walk back home, his skates hanging from his shoulder.

And then the idea struck! Home to the toolshed he ran, and there, with a hammer, pliers, and four large wooden spools, he created a new sport. By carefully fastening the spools to a pair of old shoes fitted with leather straps, he created the very first pair of roller skates.

Though the inventor of roller skating must have been excited with his new invention, it's doubtful that the skates worked very well. In fact, little more was heard about roller skating until the year 1760. At that time Joseph Merlin, a Belgian mechanic and musical-instrument maker, crafted a pair of skates that skittered along on small wheels.

Showing off his creation to a group of fascinated observers in London, Merlin quickly discovered a very serious flaw in his skates—they couldn't stop.

A local newspaper told the story of Merlin's adventure the next morning: "He flew against a mirror [worth a great deal of money], dashed it to atoms, broke his musical instrument to pieces, and wounded himself severely."

With that kind of introduction to Europe, it's not surprising that roller skating again disappeared until 1818, when skates again returned to view—this time in Berlin on a ballet stage. They made such an impression that, the following year, roller skates were being worn on the streets of Paris. The skates could travel only in a straight line, however, and stopping was difficult, at best.

Several years later, in 1863, a New York man by the name of James Plimpton redesigned the skate by replacing the easily broken wooden wheels with metal ones and installing a device that would allow the skate to turn easily by a simple shift of the skater's body weight.

Plimpton's invention created a worldwide storm of interest in roller skating and made Plimpton famous. He built a $100,000 roller skating rink in New York and organized the New York Roller Skating Association, a group that promoted the new sport of roller skating both in the United States and abroad.

Soon, roller skating rinks were sprouting up all over

the world. The sport grew into a mania. Dozens of inventors offered their own versions of Plimpton's roller skate —some undoubtedly superior, others falling far short.

After a short while, however, the roller skating mania began to die down. The main reason was that once skaters learned how to skate around the rink, they felt they had learned all there was to know. They became bored. There were no tricks they could perform, no special contests to compete in, no couples or figure skating. The rinks were too small and too crowded with single skaters skating round and round. Roller skating, too, it seemed, was going round in circles. Soon, interest dropped to nothing.

But Plimpton was a shrewd man. He realized why people had tired of roller skating, and he set about correcting the sport's shortcomings. He and other enterprising rink owners organized roller skating exhibitions, hired professional skating instructors, and encouraged figure skating.

In large cities, bigger and better rinks were built. One of the biggest of them all opened in Chicago in 1902 and for years remained a popular gathering place for skaters of all ages. More than seven thousand people turned out for the opening of the Chicago Coliseum skating rink. The following year, the old Madison Square Garden in New York converted its facilities to a roller skating rink. The Grand Central Plaza did likewise, attracting thousands of eager roller skaters.

The boom was on once again.

In 1937, a group of roller skating rink operators got together and formed the Roller Skating Rink Operators

Association of the United States (RSROA), in an effort to advance amateur roller skating in America. RSROA soon adopted a set of rules for international competition in figure, freestyle, and dance skating classes on roller skates. The first national competition to be sanctioned by the group was held in Cincinnati, Ohio, in 1938. It was a speed-skating championship, followed the next year by the first RSROA national figure and dance skating championships in Detroit, Michigan, and Mineola, New York.

In 1940, figure, speed, and dance skating championships were combined for the first time in a national competition held at the Cleveland Public Auditorium. The four-day affair attracted nearly five hundred roller skaters seeking to share in the awards.

The following year, RSROA formed a professional school, so that the nation's instructors could gather each year to exchange information and discuss skating and teaching procedures. The school also voted in rules for the game of roller hockey and regulations concerning the formation of amateur roller hockey teams and leagues.

Roller skating was fast becoming an organized sport —and a popular one. In 1958, more than 250,000 girl scouts in the United States took and passed a roller skating merit badge test, making this badge the second most popular, behind swimming.

Today, more than seventy million Americans are estimated to have roller skated at one time or another. That's nearly one out of every three American men, women, and children. Roller skating is a college course at at least two American universities—Oklahoma State and Oral Roberts.

Oklahoma State offers two college credits for successful completion of a roller skating course.

The Boy Scouts and Explorer Scouts in America think that roller skating is something special, too. A recent computer study done in Tulsa, Oklahoma, showed that nearly sixteen hundred youngsters of Explorer Scout age in that area—a fairly large proportion—listed roller skating as their number one source of enjoyment.

Shortly after that information was released, a large rink in Tulsa invited the Scouts to hold a regular Explorer get-together at the rink once a week. So far, the gatherings have been very successful.

Where is roller skating going from here? Quite far, according to the United States Amateur Confederation of Roller Skating (USAC) officials. In 1975, a major breakthrough came when roller skating was chosen as a sport for the 1979 Pan American Games. This is considered to be the first major step toward the admission of roller skating into the Olympic Games—something skating organizations have been aiming for since the early 1930s.

Early in 1977, the sport took another giant step toward Olympic participation when it received a Class A status on the United States Olympic Committee. That means roller skating now ranks with track and field, boxing, swimming, and other Class A Olympic sports and is entitled to a representative on the Board of Directors of the United States Olympic Committee. Soon roller skating competition may be part of the Olympic schedule, and young roller skaters may be competing for the coveted bronze, silver, and gold medals of the Olympics—the most highly respected of all world competitions.

It is an opportunity well deserved.

WHY SO POPULAR?

Roller skating appeals to many people for many different reasons. For one, the skates themselves are ingenious devices that allow a skater to slide across sleek, polished floors as effortlessly as ice skaters glide across a frozen pond.

Since roller skating rinks are enclosed, it's possible to skate year-round, regardless of the seasons or the weather. This appeals to both youngsters and adults interested in pleasantly passing an afternoon or evening while getting some important exercise.

The truly nice thing about roller skating is that the sport can be mildly strenuous or very exhausting. It can provide as much exercise as a brisk game of tennis or an afternoon of bicycle riding. Roller skating develops grace, balance, poise, and physical endurance. As Joseph Shev-

Over: Malisa Price shows grace, balance, and poise as she performs a spin on roller skates. But strength and fearlessness are also needed to achieve the proper height in the jump she is doing.

elson of the Roller Skating Foundation of America once wrote, "It helps the young to grow up and the older persons to regain their youth."

Another reason for roller skating's continuing popularity is that it is an easy sport to learn. The basics can be learned in a matter of minutes. But, for the serious skater, advanced techniques and figure-skating routines may take a lifetime of practice and dedication. How far you go is up to you.

2

THE MODERN-DAY SKATE

Today's roller skates are quite different from those of the past. Many new, lightweight materials have led to lighter, stronger skates that last longer and require very little maintenance.

The skate most commonly used in today's roller skating rinks is a standard skate with a shoe (called the boot) attached and loose-ball wheels carefully ground for smooth, noiseless rolling. The skate is attached to the boot by means of rivets in the plate. Some skates come with the boots attached; others are sold separately and must be attached to boots also bought separately.

Whichever type you buy, it's a good idea to buy the best skates you can afford. You can usually trade them in for a larger size when you outgrow them. Cheap, bargain-basement skates may break after a short period of use and will certainly be awkward or impossible to perform well in.

If you prefer, you can rent skates instead for a modest fee at most roller skating rinks.

THE PARTS OF A SKATE

Today's skates vary slightly from model to model or brand to brand, but most have several parts in common. Besides

the plate and boot, there is the "truck," which allows both the front and rear sets of wheels to turn without actually leaving the floor. On the truck is "action rubber," an "action screw," and an "action nut," in addition to various washers and retainers.

The wheels on most skates sold are of plastic or other man-made material, though some are of wood. Inside the wheels, encircling the axle, are ball bearings that provide quiet, nearly friction-free movement.

CARING FOR SKATES

No matter what brand of skates you buy, you should take proper care of them (including the boots) so that they will last a long time and give you good service. Check the skates carefully before each use. Make sure all nuts are tight and the trucks are set as loosely or as tightly as you wish (the looser the truck, the more easily the skate tends to turn with sideward pressure).

Spin the wheels a few times to make sure they turn freely. If they are binding, they may need a drop of oil or perhaps professional maintenance or adjustment. When this is the case, have an expert at a local rink examine the skates.

Skates may be rented from most rinks, but make sure that your rented skates fit as well as ones you would buy.

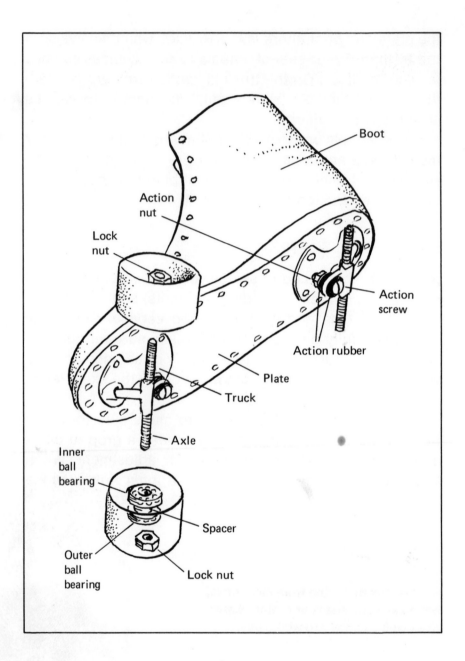

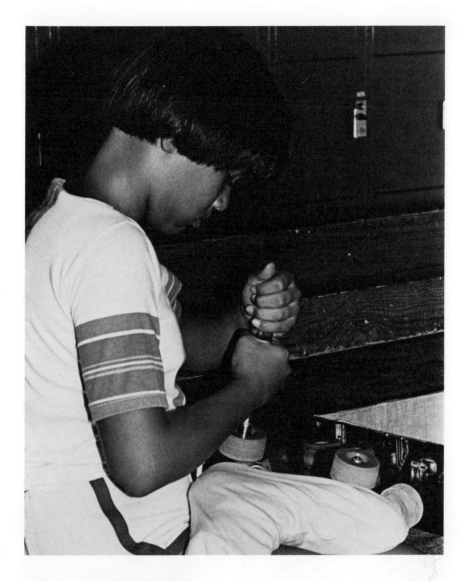

**Left, a modern roller skate.
Above, nuts on wheels must be
tightened with a special tool.**

Leather boots need some care in order to maintain their shape and to wear well over a long period of time. If boots are wet with perspiration after use, let them dry in normal room temperature. Placing the boots near a heater will cause the leather to shrink, harden, and crack.

Treat the boots to an occasional helping of a good leather preservative or conditioning oil. And, when you are not using your skates, place a shoe tree in the boots to help them retain the proper shape.

With just a little care and common sense, you should enjoy your skates for many years.

3

READY FOR ACTION

Roller skating is an easy sport to learn. But, like all new sports, it is important to learn the right way from the beginning. By learning properly, you'll avoid picking up bad habits which will be hard to unlearn later on.

To start, make sure you know how to put your skates on properly. First, unlace or loosen the laces at all eyelets. This will prevent the leather from stretching out when you insert your foot into the boot. Next, slip your foot into the boot and begin tightening the laces from the bottom up, pulling firmly above each eye. When you reach the top of the boot, pull both lace ends firmly and tie them securely in a bow. Be sure the laces are tied high enough off the floor so you won't skate over the ends and take a tumble!

Still seated, check to see that the skates feel secure without hurting. If they seem too tight, go back and loosen the laces slightly. If they feel too loose, even though the laces are tightly tied, you may need a smaller pair of skates. Skating in roller skates that are either too big or too small for your feet will be very uncomfortable. You may develop blisters that will be painful for several days after skating. Improperly fitted skates may even prevent you from skating the right way.

After both skates are on and feel secure, shake first the left, then the right one. Does anything feel loose or do you hear any peculiar rattles? If so, you should ask the expert at the rink to check it. A loose wheel can separate from the skate, dumping you in the middle of the floor! While that rarely happens, it is a problem that's easy to avoid simply by checking *before* you start out onto the floor.

HOW TO GET GOING

To roller-skate properly, you must first break an old habit —walking! Many people skating for the first time try to walk in their skates. They place one foot ahead of the other and then try to shift their weight to the forward skate. Doing this on roller skates, however, will cause the back skate to slide out behind you, while the front skate is extended. The result will be sure and painful: a quick, hard fall.

Try to readjust your thinking about how you are going to move. Think of one skate as a support skate, the other as a pushing skate. Using the railing along the side of the rink for balance, shift your weight over to the support skate (usually called the "carrying skate") while you push back on the side of the other skate (usually called the "pushing skate"). You will start to move forward.

As you bring both skates together again, shift your

The basic move.

weight to the opposite skate and push with the other skate. It is this pushing motion with the back foot that forces the wheels on the carrying skate to roll forward. And when the wheels roll forward, you move!

Remember when taking each stroke that you are not stamping your wheelprints into the floor. Do it easily, gently. Glide the skates smoothly in the direction you want to move. Practice transferring your weight smoothly from one carrying skate to the other. As you shift the weight to the new carrying skate, you may bend your knee an inch (2.5 cm) or so to help you maintain your balance and feel comfortable.

Are you skating in a perfectly straight line? If so, you're doing something wrong! Actually, you should always aim the skate either to the middle of the rink or to the rail, all the while "leaning" on one side of the skate or the other. Never aim the skate straight ahead or you will be skating on what's called a "flat." Skating on a flat is not technically correct, nor is it as easy as taking slow, semicircular sweeps to the right and then to the left.

FOLLOWING THROUGH

Tennis players, golfers, and most other athletes spend much of their time learning how to "follow through," doing something a little extra to improve their performance.

Following through is important in roller skating, too. While you can begin skating easily enough by pushing off with the side of your foot, it's much better to use the entire leg in the pushing movement. Learning how to do this may take some practice, but it will be worth it. It will make you a better, stronger skater.

The best way to begin the pushing stroke on skates is with the body upright and both knees slightly bent. The skates should be beneath the body and parallel—both facing the same way.

Begin shifting your body weight over the pushing skate and, using pressure on the inside of the pushing skate, move that skate out to the side and back. This will move the carrying skate forward. Then, slowly and steadily, shift your body weight to the carrying skate as the pushing skate is left behind.

Keep the pushing skate on the floor until the knee of that leg straightens and you can comfortably lift up the foot. When the pushing leg is lifted from the skating surface, it is called the "free leg," or "balance leg."

When you bend the knee of the balance leg and bring it alongside the other skate, the process will be repeated, with the balance skate becoming the carrying skate and the other becoming the pushing skate.

STOPPING ON SKATES

Stopping on skates is quite easy, but it will require a bit of practice and a little caution at first. It's best to start from a standing-still position.

Place the right skate behind the heel of the left one, forming a "T" position. With the body upright, bend both

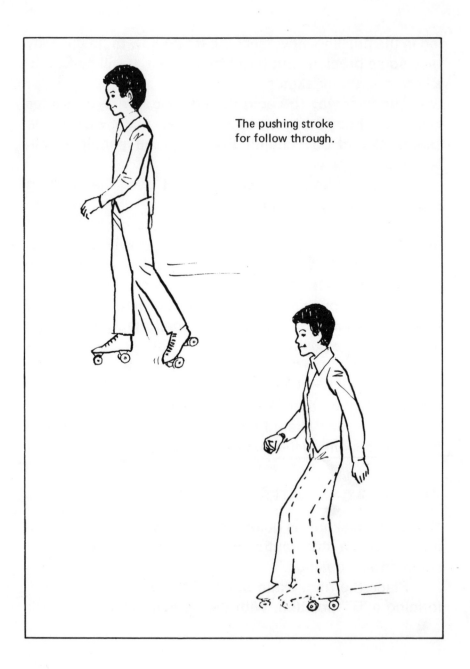

The pushing stroke
for follow through.

The T stop

knees and push off easily onto the left skate, so that you're moving forward at a slow to moderate speed.

Next, return the right skate to the "T" position, pressing the middle of the skate into the heel of the left skate. Gradually lower the right skate onto the skating surface, keeping both skates pressed together in a "T," and transfer your body weight to the right skate. The friction, or rubbing, of the right skate on the skating surface will act as a brake, stopping your movement.

You'll notice a slight tendency to lunge forward while stopping. You can resist this by supporting your body with a firm, straight back and leaning slightly against the direction you're moving in until the skate brings you to a stop.

AIMING AND STEERING
THE SKATES

A roller skate has no steering wheel. If you skate far enough, you'll either have to turn or stop—or run right into the wall, as Joseph Merlin did so many years ago!

How does a person turn on skates? By leaning the body in the direction of the turn. This applies "leverage," or extra weight, to the action rubber mounted on the skates' trucks, which in turn changes the "pitch" of the wheels and makes the skate follow a curved path in the direction you lean. This path is called an "edge." It's the way good skaters travel around the rink.

When a skater leans away from the balance leg, or free leg, the skater is said to be using an "outside edge." When the skater leans into the direction of the balance leg, he or she is using an "inside edge."

Skating on an outside edge.

Skating on an inside edge.

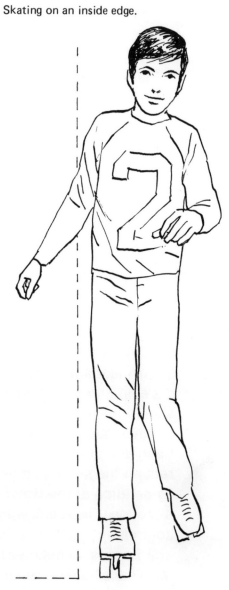

The lean.

In leaning to the side in order to turn, some skaters develop the bad habit of bending from the waist. You should always apply pressure to the skate while keeping a firm, straight upper body. The hips and shoulders should be in line at all times and the body squarely set in the direction the skate is moving. Never try to force your leans by bending at the waist and pulling your skate into a new direction. The result would be poor balance and little edge control.

Lean is sometimes hard for beginning skaters to master. That's because ever since you learned to walk upright, your body has been in an upright position—a natural position that your body muscles hold even when you're not thinking about it.

When you suddenly get on skates and start to lean to one side or the other, the muscles automatically try to adjust the body to an upright position.

Practice is the best way to get used to leaning while moving around the floor on skates. Just be sure your body is leaning straight from neck to knees—not bent from the waist.

When the entire body is used to apply pressure to the side of the skate, very little lean is necessary, even to turn the sharpest arc or curve. Don't overlean or you'll topple off your skates. Begin the lean gradually. When you have achieved the proper lean, you will feel your turns taking place almost naturally.

SKATING BALANCE
AND POSTURE

The most important part of skating well is achieving correct balance. When you walk, one leg goes out ahead of the body.

The opposite is true in skating. The leg that's off the floor (the balance leg) must go back to provide a push for the other leg (the carrying skate). Meanwhile, the balance leg helps to maintain your balance.

Your weight should rest more over the middle or the ball of your foot than back on the heel, which could make you fall. Your body should also be erect, with your back firm. Practice keeping your head up (you don't have to watch your skates for them to work!) and your eyes straight ahead. Besides looking more sure of yourself and more graceful, you won't run into anybody!

SKATING BACKWARD

After you become good at skating forward, you will probably want to try skating backward. If you can skate forward, learning this new movement will be easy. The balance that you learned in skating forward will be used to help you skate backward. The rules of balance and movement are nearly the same.

The Scissors Stroke
Using the scissors stroke is the best way to begin moving backward on skates. Scissors will help you maintain your balance because you must keep both skates on the floor at all times.

To start, stand straight, with no bending at the waist. Balance your body weight evenly over the balls of both feet. Bend your knees slightly and hold the feet so that the toes are pointed in a bit.

While exerting pressure on the inside wheels of both skates, push the two skates a small distance apart while

Proper balance is the key to enjoyable skating. The boy on the left of the picture obviously hasn't achieved it yet.

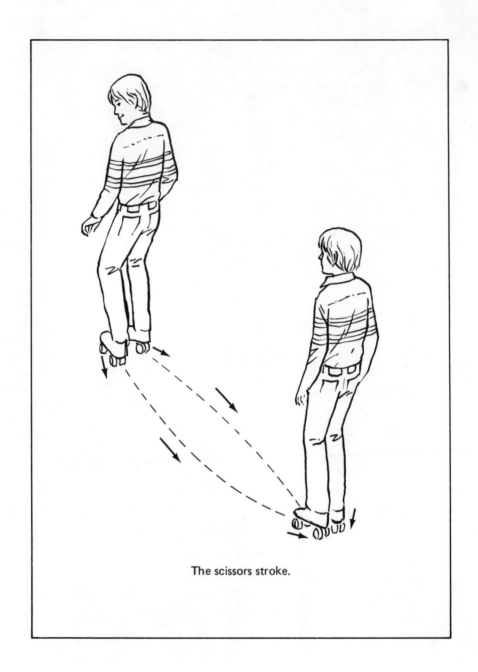

The scissors stroke.

keeping both on the floor. You've moved a small distance backward! Once the skates are apart a few inches (6 cm), return them to the position where the heels are pointing inward, still maintaining pressure on the inside edges of both skates and keeping them both on the floor. Now you've completed one scissors cycle.

Repeat the steps above until you can maintain a steady in-and-out motion for several minutes at a time.

Be sure in doing this movement that you don't allow the skates to drift too far apart. A few inches (6 cm) is all that's necessary. Also, as the heels come in, don't let them touch, or you will stop your backward motion and may even fall.

Raising the Skates

After mastering the scissors motion in backward skating, you'll be ready to try one-foot backward skating, that is, lifting the skates as in forward skating.

Begin by working up a little backward speed using the scissors motion, then lift each skate alternately, one after the other. The pushing skate will become the balance leg as the foot leaves the floor and moves to the front of the body, with the toe held down and close to the floor.

When you return the balance leg to the floor alongside the carrying skate, be sure the foot is under control. Then repeat the backward stroke with the other skate.

Once you've tried this method of backward skating, you'll be surprised at how easy it is—and how quickly you can become a really good backward skater.

THE MOHAWK TURN

Once you've learned to skate both forward and backward, you should learn the Mohawk, or eagle, turn. This turn will enable you to move from one direction to the other without coming to a complete stop.

The Mohawk turn requires both skates to be placed in a single line, heel to heel, with the toes pointing outward in opposite directions.

While in this position, commonly called "spread eagle," one skate will be moving forward, the other backward. If you have trouble with the position, you may have to work at it, either on or off skates, until your legs are more flexible.

As you are moving forward on skates, place your weight solidly over your right skate (the carrying skate). Stand erect, with the hip of your left leg (balance, or free, leg) carried level with the other hip.

Rotate or turn your left (free) leg and skate outward, toward your right. The left skate should be carried close to the floor. Drop this skate, with the toe aimed backward, onto the skating surface, near the heel of the right skate. Immediately shift your weight from the right to the left

Skating backward is easier than it looks. Here, Malisa is moving quite fast. To keep her balance, she is bent deeply at the waist and has her arms stretched out in front of her.

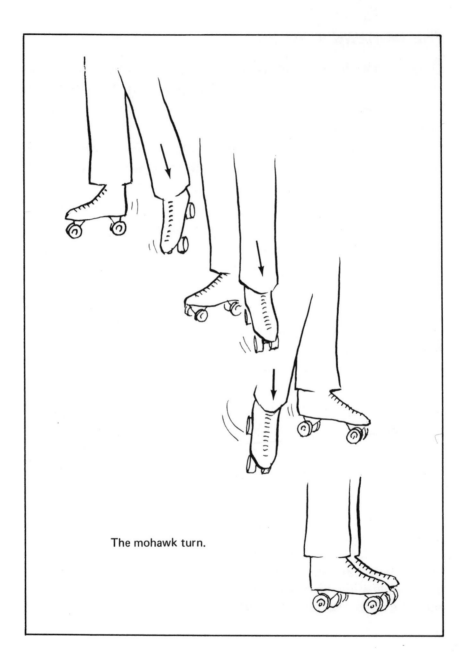

The mohawk turn.

skate, lift your right skate from the floor, and bring it to rest on the skating surface alongside the left skate.

This is the trickiest part of the turn—the transfer of weight from right to left skate. If your weight is still on the right skate when you go to lift it up, you'll fall. Be sure before doing the lifting that your weight has shifted completely to the left skate.

Once you successfully learn to do that, you'll have learned to skate from a forward to a backward skating position. To return to skating forward, repeat the process of the Mohawk turn in reverse.

WIPING OUT

No matter how carefully you try to skate, sooner or later you are going to fall. While falling rarely causes serious damage, there are some steps you can take to soften the blow.

While learning to skate, wear heavy pants or jeans. Usually, skaters who fall land on their knees. Without some sort of protection, bruises, skinned knees, or even cuts may result.

When you feel yourself losing your balance, don't fight to stay on your feet. Try to fall as easily as possible. Use your hands extended at your sides to help absorb some of the impact of the fall.

Once on the floor, get into a comfortable half-kneeling position with your left knee on the floor and the wheels of your right skate on the floor next to it. Concentrate your weight over your right skate and slowly raise yourself up

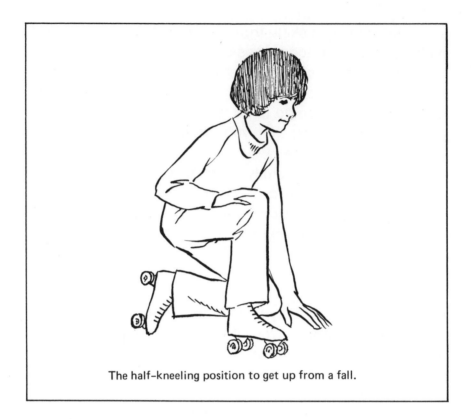

The half-kneeling position to get up from a fall.

by straightening that knee and bringing the other foot alongside.

You may feel foolish the first few times you fall. But you'll soon realize that *all* skaters fall from time to time. Even the experts doing advanced steps lose their balance and go down. It's nothing to be ashamed of. Simply get up, dust yourself off, and start all over again.

Remember: the more you work at it, the less you'll fall. Falling is usually the result of not having good balance. As you get used to your skates, your sense of balance will steadily improve.

4
SKATING PARTIES, GAMES, AND CONTESTS

Skating alone is fun. Skating with a group of friends is even more fun. Besides enjoying the sport of roller skating, you can enjoy the company of your friends and share your fun with them.

One way to have fun skating with a group is to throw a skating party. To have a party, you'll need the services of a nearby skating rink. Rink time can often be rented for supervised parties that include games, competitions, refreshments, and open skating.

What games can be played on roller skates? Some of the more popular ones follow.

HOKEY-POKEY

"You put your left foot in, you put your left foot out, you put your left foot in, and you shake it all about. You do the hokey-pokey and you turn yourself around. That's what it's all about."

These are the words to an old familiar song. To play the hokey-pokey game on skates, have the skaters form a circle facing inward. Go through the motions of the song, using left foot, right foot, left elbow, right elbow, head, backside, and finally the whole self for the various verses. Everyone should sing and slap their knees, clap their hands, or snap their fingers to "That's what it's all about."

The winner is the person who seems the loosest. He or she should receive a "Loosest Participant" ribbon to wear for the rest of the party, or be given the title "Head Hokey" and receive a special award at the snack bar.

Hokey-pokey records may be obtained at most record shops.

PASS THE FOOTBALL

For this version of "hot potato," several small, lightweight balls are used. The skaters must pass or throw the balls to their right while the music is playing. At the instant the music stops or a whistle blows, whoever has his or her hands on the hot "football" is out of the game and leaves the floor. The last remaining skater wins a prize.

MUSICAL PLATES

A variation of the old "musical chairs" game can be played with paper plates. Place the plates around the rink —one less than the total number of players. When the music stops, the skaters must skate to the nearest plate (only one person to a plate!). The person unable to get to a plate must leave the floor. The winner is the last remaining player.

For a fun variation, musical plates can be played with couples. When the music stops, the couples must skate to the plates without breaking hand contact.

BALLOON BLAST RELAY

This fun game offers thrills and the chance to improve skating skills. Each team consists of four or five contestants who all line up. The first skater on each team races to the opposite end of the rink, breaks a balloon by sitting on it, and then goes back to the end of his or her team line. Then the next member of the team starts on the relay lap, and so on. The winning team is the one that breaks all its balloons and returns "home" first.

MOVE-UP COUPLES

This is a popular boy-meets-girl skating game that begins as couples pair up in double columns—boys on the inside and girls on the outside. Each time the whistle sounds, the boys move up one and skate with the girls alongside.

Several competitive skating contests can also be staged. Aside from being fun, they will help you to develop better skating form. These contests are for skaters who already have good balance. Groups may range in size from six to twelve or more contestants.

THE SLALOM

Props needed: Fourteen paper plates, cone markers or similar objects; stopwatch.

Objective: To skate a zigzag course without touching or knocking over any obstacles. By changing the placement of the obstacles, this event can be made more or less difficult. The winner is the skater who crosses the finish line in the fastest time. Touching an obstacle adds 5 seconds to the total score.

SHOOT-THE-DUCK SLALOM

Props needed: Fourteen paper plates, cone markers, or similar objects; stopwatch.

Objective: To skate a course past the plates while in a sitting position. From a rolling start, the skaters enter the starting gate in a shoot-the-duck position. Plates may be placed closer or farther apart to make the slalom more or less difficult. The winner is the skater who crosses the finish line in the fastest time. Touching an obstacle adds 5 seconds to the total score.

**Malisa demonstrates the
shoot-the-duck position.**

SHUTTLE SKATE

Props needed: Six paper plates; two wooden blocks or similar objects for each skater; stopwatch.

Objective: To race to the first plate and pick up a block, race to the second plate and deposit the block, race to the third plate and pick up a block, race to the fourth plate and deposit the block, then race back to the starting line. For each block not picked up or not placed on the plate, 5 seconds are added. The winner is the skater who completes the skate in the fastest time.

CRISSCROSS

Props needed: A masking-tape line (or one already painted line) at least 20 feet (6 m) long.

Objective: To zigzag back and forth across the line as many times as possible without stopping. The winner is the person who completes the most zigzags on the traffic line. Each time a skater stops or touches the floor with body or hands, 1 point is deducted from the score.

5
COMPETITIVE SKATING

Those just learning to skate sometimes wonder how long it takes to become really good. The answer to that question depends on a variety of factors: for example, age, physical strength, coordination, amount of qualified instruction, type and quality of equipment, and the number of times a week the skater skates.

Top competitive skaters usually begin skating at an early age. By the time they are fourteen or fifteen years old, they are in excellent physical condition. Usually they roller-skate for an hour or more each day. Their equipment is often the best that money can buy. The results are a national or world championship . . . maybe.

Competitive skaters do not begin competing at the top. Every national champion started at a lower level of competition.

Most skaters begin skating when their parents start taking them once a week or so to the local rink for a little exercise and some fun. Before very long, some skaters decide they want to learn more complicated moves, and so enroll in lessons—either private or group—taught by the skating rink "pro."

The pro's job is to teach advanced skating techniques to skaters of all ages. If a young skater works hard and shows promise, the pro may decide to enter him or her in competition.

A skater entering competition for the first time must join a competitive skating club. In the United States, both the skater and the club must be registered with the USAC in order to participate in sanctioned—official—competition. Your instructor or local rink director will tell you how to join.

The first competition you will probably enter will be a small, interclub contest held on a local scale. There you can expect to compete against ten or more other skaters from the area matched to your own degree of skating skill.

After the local competition, the rink pro might decide you are ready for an invitational meet—usually a larger contest than the local event and offering more competition.

Every spring, each of the fifty states in the United States holds its own state meet. Though anyone may enter, usually the rink pros around the state decide which skaters are ready for the tougher competition. Winners at the state level may then be ready to compete in Regional Meets.

The top three skaters in each division of the Regional Meets qualify for the National Artistic Competition. At the Nationals, the top three skaters in International Dance, In-

Malisa works on the routine
she will do at an
upcoming skating contest.

ternational Figures, International Freestyle, and Pairs categories qualify for world competition. It's a long, long way from that first local contest to a world competition, but it's an exciting journey.

Outside the United States, such as in Great Britain, skaters are usually entered into competitions according to age and skill. Skaters who have not passed any skills tests and are under thirteen years of age are usually entered in what are called Novice Class events. Skaters under the age of thirteen who have passed certain tests may enter the Primary Championship Class events. Skaters who have passed certain tests, but are below sixteen years of age, may enter Intermediate Class events. Finally, experienced and qualified skaters may enter the National Class events. At all these levels of competition skaters compete for a variety of cups in events such as Roller Dance, Roller Pair skating, and Roller Figure skating. There is usually an entry fee, which varies according to what class the skater enters.

Most young skaters interested in competing have begun skating by the age of eight. Usually, they enter speed rather than artistic contests because it's an easier category. While speed skating requires physical stamina, artistic skating is an exacting, trying art in which the competition is keen.

It may take a hard-working skater three years of competing to make it to a national competition, although a lot

Coach Tony Wipperfurth of the Rollerdrome in Madison, Wisconsin, helps Malisa with a difficult move.

The position shown above, called the camel, is often used in artistic competition, and requires excellent balance and form. Right, to help her achieve grace and flexibility, Malisa takes ballet lessons, too. She then does many of the ballet movements on skates.

depends on what part of the country the skater lives in. A competitor from the Northwest United States would have an easier time making it to the national championships than one from the more populated Northeast. The same is true at the state level of competition. A skater from a low-population state such as Wyoming or Idaho would have an easier time winning a state championship than one from New York or Pennsylvania.

Is competition worth all the time and effort necessary to advance through the various levels? Most competitors feel it is. Even those who enter and fail to win say the experience of competition, as well as the chance to watch excellent skaters in action and to meet new friends, is well worth every hour of practice.

There is another form of competition in roller skating —one quite different from speed and artistic skating. It's a more specialized, often more exciting form that combines the quickness of track with the power of football and the finesse of dance. It's called puck hockey, and it's played on wheels.

The object of puck hockey is the same as that of ice hockey: to guide a puck around the rink using only sticks and skates and to shoot the puck into the goal for a score. The game is divided into three periods, with a

**Pair dancing on skates
is an exacting art and requires
a great deal of training.**

short intermission between each action-packed segment of play.

Players in puck hockey are allowed a certain amount of body contact, called checking. But if a player gets too rough or uses an illegal move, he or she may be called for a penalty by the official. That player must then sit out several minutes of the game while the rest of the team plays on.

As in ice hockey, puck hockey features more than brute force and fast skating. There is quite a bit of strategy involved. Players must pass accurately from one to another, set up plays, and perform all the other tactics that have made hockey so popular over the last few years.

Another form of hockey on wheels is every bit as exciting as puck hockey. It is called ball hockey and is identical except that a ball is used instead of a puck.

Both puck and ball hockey competitions offer girls as well as boys a chance to compete.

INDEX

ABOUT THE AUTHOR

D. J. Herda is a free-lance writer who has to his credit nine books, two plays, and over one thousand short stories and articles in a variety of national magazines and newspapers. He currently also writes a syndicated column on photography, a special interest of his. D. J. lives in Madison, Wisconsin.